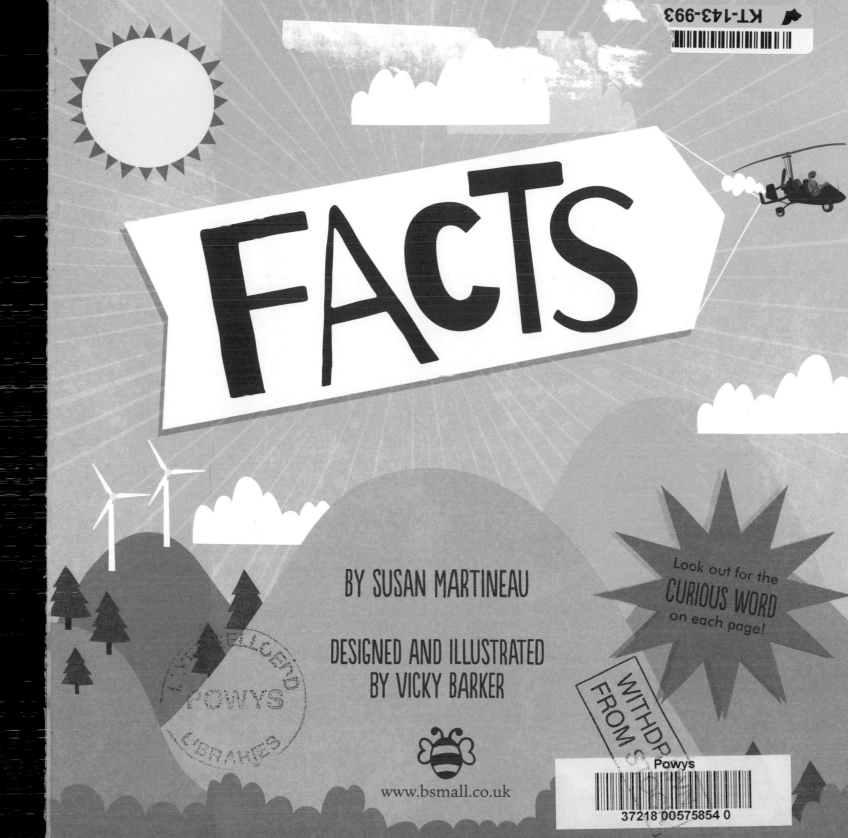

FACTS

BY SUSAN MARTINEAU

DESIGNED AND ILLUSTRATED
BY VICKY BARKER

Look out for the
CURIOUS WORD
on each page!

www.bsmall.co.uk

Published by b small publishing ltd. www.bsmall.co.uk © b small publishing ltd. 2015 • 1 2 3 4 5 • ISBN 978-1-909767-73-7 •
Production by Madeleine Ehm. Printed in China by WKT Co. Ltd.

GREEN THINGS IN THE RAINFOREST

EMERALD TREE BOA

When this snake is young it is not green but reddish-orange. It stays up in the trees where it feeds on rats, lizards and monkeys.

TROPICAL RAINFOREST

This grows around the central part of the Earth. It is always hot and humid and contains an amazing variety of plants and animals.

GREAT GREEN MACAW

Macaws are the biggest of the world's parrots. They use their strong, hooked beaks to crack nuts and seeds.

WHITE-LIPPED TREE FROG

This frog can be bright green or brownish green, but it always has a white bottom lip. It has big feet with large webbed toes and is a fantastic tree-climber. Male frogs can also bark like a dog!

PRAYING MANTIS

This bug looks like an alien with its triangular head and massive eyes. Its spiky front legs are folded so that it looks as if it is praying.

TUCUNARE FISH

This fierce fish is a really determined hunter. It does not give up, even if it misses its prey the first time around. Then it usually swallows it whole.

CURIOUS WORD

ARBOREAL

means 'living up in trees'.
It is very handy to be
an arboreal creature if
you are in a rainforest.

GREEN TREE PYTHON

The tail of this python
is a different colour to
its body. The snake can
wiggle it to make it
look like a worm
to attract prey.

MADAGASCAN GIANT DAY GECKO

A vivid green gecko with patches of red on
its back or head. It lives in Madagascar, a
rainforest island off the coast of Africa.
It can be up to 25 cm (10 inches) long.

EXPLORER'S HAMMOCK

The most comfy way to sleep
in the rainforest. The best
hammocks have built-in bug
netting to protect you too.

RAINFOREST LEAVES

Most of the leaves on the
trees in the rainforest have
a shiny surface so that
heavy rain slides
off easily.

AMAZONIAN WATER LILY

The leaves of this plant can
grow to over 2.5 metres (8 feet)
across. They are so strong that a
baby could sit on one.

AT HOME IN SPACE

INTERNATIONAL SPACE STATION

A working laboratory that is home to astronauts from many different countries. It is bigger than a six-bedroomed house and orbits 386 km (240 miles) above Earth.

SPACEWALK

This is when an astronaut goes outside the space station to repair something or to carry out an experiment. A space walk usually lasts between five to eight hours depending on the job that needs doing.

STRAPS AND FASTENINGS

Everything, even really heavy objects, floats in the space station because the force of gravity that normally pulls things down to Earth is not very strong in space. Straps, fastenings and Velcro are essential to keep things where you can find them.

VIEW FROM SPACE

The crew can see the sun setting and rising 16 times a day as the space station orbits the Earth once every 90 minutes. The views are spectacular.

SPACE MEALS

Food is ready to eat from specially prepared packages. No plates are needed. Sometimes a cargo vehicle brings in fresh fruit, but there's no pizza delivery in space!

MICROGRAVITY

means that even heavy things seem not to weigh anything and people and objects can float around. There is only a small ('micro') amount of gravity in a space station that is orbiting, or going round, the Earth.

SPACE POTTY

This is a suction-system toilet that works like a vacuum cleaner to make sure everything gets sucked into a waste tank. It is still very important to aim well!

CREW CABIN

Each astronaut has a tiny cabin that can fit just one person. Sleeping-bags have to be hooked to the wall so they don't float off.

URINE FUNNEL

This yellow funnel catches pee that is then recycled into clean water. Water is very precious in space.

DRINKS IN SPACE

Astronauts drink out of watertight containers with straws to prevent any drops escaping. Water droplets are very dangerous inside the space station as they can float around and damage equipment.

EXERCISE

Bones can get very weak in space so the crew must exercise for at least two hours every day to keep them strong.

ANIMALS ON DUTY

DOG DETECTIVES

Sniffer dogs are trained to find illegal drugs, guns, explosives or blood at crime scenes. Search dogs are used to find missing people and bodies.

MEDAL WINNERS

The Dickin Medal is a special award for animal bravery in wartime. Since 1943 it has been awarded to 32 pigeons (used as messengers), 29 dogs, three horses and Simon the cat.

PDSA

For

Gallantry

WE ALSO SERVE

WAR DOGS

Dogs have been used in wartime since ancient times. Sergeant Stubby, a Boston Bull Terrier, is said to have captured a spy during World War One!

SIMON THE CAT

Simon was the Captain's cat on HMS *Amethyst* during World War Two. Even though he was wounded, he kept everyone cheerful during a terrible attack.

HUNTING WITH EAGLES

The Kazakh people of western Mongolia use golden eagles to hunt for foxes and hares. They train them when they are little eaglets, but always return them to the wild after a few years of hunting together.

CURIOUS WORD ➛

DOMESTICATED

is used to describe pets or other animals that are trained to live or work for humans.

DOCTOR RAT

In Tanzania in Africa they have trained rats to sniff human spit to see if a person has a nasty illness called tuberculosis. The rats can do it in minutes and this means the person can be helped straightaway.

SNIFFING SKILLS

Dogs can help scientists find threatened species like bumblebees. They can also sniff out cancer in humans and let people with diabetes know when they need their medicine.

MEDICAL ALERT DOG

BLOODSUCKERS

Leeches like to suck the blood of mammals, including humans. Doctors can use them to create a good flow of blood when skin is grafted from one part of the body to an injured part.

SEA MAMMAL MINESWEEPERS

The US Navy uses dolphins and sea lions to find and mark suspicious objects in the ocean, like mines (bombs in the sea). Dolphins use their echolocation skill and sea lions are really good at seeing in dark, murky waters.

BEST-FRIEND DOGS

Guide dogs are trained to help blind people at home and when they are out and about. Hearing dogs will nudge or put a paw on a deaf person to alert them to noises like the telephone, doorbell or an alarm.

BRAVE EXPLORERS OF THE WORLD

AMELIA EARHART

She was known as the 'Winged Legend'. In 1932 she became the first woman to fly across the Atlantic on her own. But in 1937 she disappeared while making an attempt to fly round the world.

JOHN CABOT

In 1497 Cabot and his sons set off in a tiny ship called the *Matthew* with just 18 men. They sailed from Bristol, England to the American coast, probably landing at Cape Breton in Nova Scotia. At first Cabot thought it was China!

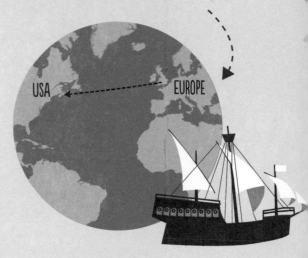

THOR HEYERDAHL

He wanted to prove that Indians from South America could have sailed to the Polynesian islands in the Pacific. In 1947 he set off in a simple wooden raft called the *Kon-Tiki*. He made it despite shark attacks and fresh water running out.

ROALD AMUNDSEN

The Norwegian polar explorer was not only the first person to reach the South Pole in 1911, but he also found a route from the Arctic Ocean to the Pacific Ocean called the Northwest Passage.

JACQUES PICCARD AND DON WALSH

They became the first people to reach the deepest-known part of the ocean in their special submarine called a bathyscaphe. In 1960 they went 7 miles down (10,915 metres) to Challenger Deep in the Mariana Trench of the Pacific Ocean.

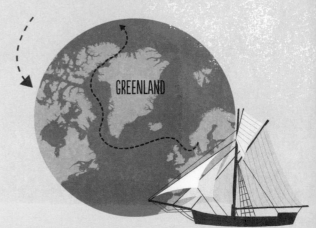

FERDINAND MAGELLAN

The Portuguese explorer set out in 1519 with five ships and about 260 men. Only one ship and 18 men made it all the way round the world, arriving home three years later in 1522. Sadly, Magellan himself did not survive the trip.

NORTH AMERICA

EUROPE

ASIA

AFRICA

OCEANIA

SOUTH AMERICA

NIGERIA

GERMAN CAMEROON

MARY KINGSLEY

During 1893 and 1894 this intrepid woman roamed the forests of the Congo in West Africa on foot and paddled up the river in a dug-out canoe. She collected specimens for the Natural History Museum in London.

Route on foot

Route by canoe

FRENCH CONGO

YURI GAGARIN

He was the first human to journey into space. On 12 April 1961 his spaceship *Vostok* was launched from Russia. It took Gagarin one hour and 48 minutes to fly right round the Earth.

BURKE AND WILLS

In 1860 Robert Burke and William Wills set out to cross Australia from south to north. They reached the swamps of the north coast, but had to turn round as their supplies were running out. Sadly they both died on the journey back.

AUSTRALIA

MELBOURNE

CURIOUS WORD

CIRCUMNAVIGATE

means to travel all the way round something, in this case the world.

CASTLE UNDER SIEGE

SIEGE

Castles were the home of a lord and his family and followers, but they also had to be strong, stone fortresses to fight off enemies. An attack on a castle was called a siege. Sieges could last for a very long time.

BATTLEMENTS

These had crenels (gaps) and merlons (the solid bits) so that people defending the castle could shoot and chuck things at attackers through the crenels and hide behind the merlons.

BAILEY

Castles were like a small village inside their huge walls. The bailey was a courtyard. It might have animals, stables and buildings for making bread and beer. This was very important during a siege when no supplies would be able to get in.

GARRISON

The soldiers who defended the castle were called a garrison. They would be armed with crossbows and longbows.

TREBUCHET

This was also known as a siege machine. It was like an enormous catapult with a swinging arm that could launch giant blocks of stone to smash into the castle. Sometimes dead animals were fired into the castle to try and spread disease.

PORTCULLIS

This heavy wooden gate in the gatehouse was made even stronger with iron. It was lowered to shut the castle off from attackers. Enemy soldiers would try to smash their way through the door using a battering ram.

THE KEEP

Also known as the great tower, this would be seen from miles around and told everyone how powerful the lord was.

LORD AND LADY'S BEDCHAMBER

The lord and his family would have private rooms in the main tower or keep. Everyone else in the castle would sleep where they worked or in the great hall.

GREAT HALL

This was the centre of life in the castle. It was where people ate, welcomed guests and where the servants slept. It was usually on one floor of the keep.

GARDEROBE

This was the loo! Soldiers might even attack a castle by climbing up the shaft of a garderobe that opened on to the outside of the castle walls into the moat.

MOAT

The moat was a deep ditch filled with water. It surrounded the castle and would slow attackers down. Enemies would fill the moat with stones and tree trunks to get across.

CURIOUS WORD

FORTIFICATION

means a wall or other strong structure built to defend a place against attack.

CLEVER CAMOUFLAGE

PRETEND TO BE DEAD

The oakleaf butterfly looks just like a dead leaf when it folds its wings. Even the veins underneath look like those on a leaf. No wonder its other name is dead-leaf butterfly!

CAMOUFLAGE

Most wild creatures are difficult to see because their shape or colour helps them blend into where they live. Camouflage can help animals to hide from predators or to hunt for prey.

FAKE WASP

The wasp beetle pretends to be a wasp with its black and yellow warning stripes. It is handy for protection to look fiercer than you are.

INVISIBLE TOAD

Frogs and toads in the rainforest have to be able to hide from hungry predators. The Asian horned toad can blend in with its surroundings on a bed of rotting leaves.

HIDDEN FAWN

Newborn baby deer have markings on their coats to look like sunlight coming through the leaves in a forest. They keep very still so predators cannot see them.

SPOTTY SHARK

The spotted wobbegong is a type of carpet shark that is flat and patterned pale yellow or greenish brown with spots. This is superb camouflage for lurking on all types of seabed. It will give you a nasty bite if you step on it!

MIMICRY

is when a creature pretends to be something else to protect itself or to find prey.

ARCTIC FUR

The beautiful arctic fox is dark in the summer and white in the winter snows. Its thick fur even covers the soles of its feet.

SHIMMERING STRIPES

When zebras stand together they are a confusing mass of black and white patterns that make it difficult for a lion to nab one! In the shimmering heat haze of Africa the zebra's stripes blur.

Tiger

INVISIBLE CATS

Tigers, jaguars, ocelots and leopards are all members of the cat family with beautiful camouflage markings. They can blend in with their surroundings to hunt their prey.

Ocelot

COLOUR-CHANGE CUTTLEFISH

These are masters of disguise and can change their colour and even the texture of their skin to match different types of seabed. They can even disguise themselves as clumps of floating seaweed!

Jaguar

Leopard

DIGGING INTO ANCIENT TIMES

MIGHTY MESOPOTAMIA

Mesopotamia, or the 'cradle of civilization', was where Iraq is now. Over 5,000 years ago this is where people first started building towns, making laws and using inventions like the wheel and writing.

SUMERIAN MASTER BUILDERS

The Sumerians were the first people to settle in Mesopotamia. They became rich from farming and built huge temples called ziggurats where they would worship their gods.

ANCIENT EGYPTIAN GAME

The Ancient Egyptians enjoyed board games. The most popular one was a bit like chess and called senet. The winner was believed to be protected by the gods. Senet sets have been found in the tombs of pharaohs.

PHOENICIAN TRADERS

The Phoenicians were expert sailors who lived around the shores of the Mediterranean Sea. They travelled around trading gold, jewels, wine, spices and glass in their large ships.

GREEK SCHOOLS

In Ancient Greece only boys went to school. From scenes painted on pottery we can see that they would use a pointed stick, called a stylus, to scratch their lessons on a wax tablet.

ANCIENT CHINESE EMPEROR

The first emperor of China, Qin Shi Huang, brought in standard versions of coins, writing and laws across the land. He also left behind an amazing tomb containing thousands of clay soldiers.

ROMAN ARMY TRICKS

The Romans had the best army in the world. Writings from the time describe one of their battle techniques called the testudo (Latin for 'tortoise'). The soldiers locked their shields together to protect themselves.

CURIOUS WORD →

ARCHAEOLOGIST

is someone who looks at ancient objects and buildings to find out how people lived in the past. They are like history detectives looking for clues.

MINOAN CRAFTSMEN

The Minoans lived on the Mediterranean island of Crete. You can still visit the remains of one of their palaces called Knossos. Minoans made beautiful wall paintings, pottery and gold jewellery.

MYSTERIOUS OLMECS OF MEXICO

The Olmecs are probably one of the earliest civilizations of Central America. They came before the Mayans and Aztecs. They carved huge stone heads and strange sculptures combining jaguars with human babies.

VIKING EXPLORATION

Archaeologists can see from the remains of their boats that Viking ships were light and could travel quickly. Vikings were the first people from Europe to sail across the Atlantic Ocean to North America, reaching Canada over a thousand years ago.

FANTASTIC FLYING MACHINES

INFLATABLE AIRSHIP

An American inventor called Charles Ritchel made the first inflatable airship or dirigible. The pilot sat under a huge bag of gas, turned a hand-crank to make the propeller work and steered using pedals.

MONSTER BALLOON

In 1783, in front of the King of France, the Montgolfier brothers launched a hot-air balloon carrying the first living beings. A duck, a sheep and a rooster flew in a small basket under the balloon.

OTTO'S GLIDER

Otto Lilienthal was a German engineer who invented a wing-flapping glider. He made several successful flights between 1891 and 1896, but sadly died after crashing in 1896.

THE FLYING MONK

In 1010 a monk called Eilmer of Malmesbury made a pair of wings. He attached them to his hands and feet and tried to fly by jumping from a high tower. He managed to go about 200 metres (650 feet) before falling down and breaking both his legs. Ow!

MAD MULTIPLANES

In the early 1900s many inventors came up with the idea of multi-winged aeroplanes, but most of them would barely leave the ground.

FLYING SAUCER

The American space agency NASA has been working on a saucer-shaped, rocket-powered space vehicle that will help in future missions to Mars. Its proper name is a Low-density Supersonic Decelerator!

CURIOUS WORD ⤵

AERONAUTICS

is the science of designing and building aircraft.

MOTORBIKES IN THE SKY

Gyrocopters look like a cross between a motorbike and a helicopter. They can fly lower than most other flying machines and land in very small spaces.

HOT-AIR HISTORY

In 1999 Bertrand Piccard and Brian Jones became the first men to fly around the world in a hot-air balloon. It took them just under 20 days in their amazing high-altitude Breitling Orbiter 3.

WINGSUITS

Modern wingsuits were first invented in the 1990s. They are also called squirrel or birdmen suits. They are very difficult to control and fliers must use a parachute to land safely.

FLYING CAR

The Hall Flying Automobile or Convair 118 was a family car with a plane on top! It did take to the air in 1947, but was wrecked on its third flight.

FORCES IN ACTION

FORCE

A force is a push or a pull. Every day we use force in many different ways. When you push or pull open a door you are applying a force. We use force when we are lifting, bending, stretching or squeezing things.

FORCES IN BALANCE

Forces come in pairs. When a force pushes on something, another one pushes back. The second force is the same strength as the first one. When you lean on a wall your weight pushes on the wall. At the same time the wall is pushing back. Otherwise you would fall through the wall!

FORCE AND MOVEMENT

Force makes things move. It will make things move faster, more slowly, or change direction. When you kick a ball or hit it with a bat you are applying a force.

GRAVITY AND WEIGHT

Gravity is a force that pulls things towards the ground. Gravity pulling us down gives us, and everything around us, weight. When we drop something it is gravity that makes it fall to the ground. When rockets blast off into space they have to go at incredible speeds to break free of the Earth's gravity.

CENTRIPETAL

is the name given to the force that stops you falling out of your seat when you are on a roller coaster looping the loop. Centripetal force keeps you pressed into your chair.

GRIPPING FORCE

The force produced when two things rub together is called friction. It is a gripping force that is often helpful. Without friction our feet would slip all over the floor and we would fall over. Too much friction can stop machines working. Oil is added to parts of machines to make less friction between the parts that need to work smoothly together.

AIR FRICTION

If you throw a ball up into the air it has to slide through the air. This causes friction too. This kind of friction is called air resistance. Air resistance can be useful if you are falling to Earth with a parachute, as it will slow you down!

FRICTION AND BIKES!

You need force to make your bike work. Friction helps you and also slows you down.

Friction between the bike and the air slows you down, especially on a windy day!

Friction between brakes and wheels makes the brakes work.

Friction helps your feet grip the pedals.

Friction between the tyres and the road helps the wheels to grip, but friction also slows the wheels down.

FRIENDLY DINOSAURS

DIPLODOCUS

This dinosaur was as long as three London buses and it had a very long neck and whip-like tail. It must have had a huge stomach to fit in all the food it needed to keep going.

BRACHIOSAURUS

This dino was built like a huge giraffe. In fact, it was taller than three giraffes and could eat from the tops of the tallest trees.

HYPSILOPHODON

This was a type of dinosaur known as an ornithopod, which means 'bird foot'. It had a horned beak and ran on two legs and moved about in herds for protection.

CAMARASAURUS

This dino had very strong jaws and spoon-shaped teeth that were useful for eating even the toughest plants. It also had stones, or gastroliths, in its stomach to help grind up food.

CURIOUS WORD ⟶

MEGAHERBIVORES

are huge, plant-eating creatures like the largest of the dinosaurs.

THERIZONOSAURUS

These long-necked dinosaurs were really tall with massive, razor-like claws more than 50 cm (19 inches) long. Scientists think these were for grabbing branches or digging up tasty roots.

TRICERATOPS

This dino had a gigantic skull with a frill of bone and three horns. Some specimens have been found with skulls nearly 3 metres (10 feet) long. It also had stacks of teeth and a beak that was good for gobbling up plants.

STEGOSAURUS

Its name means 'plated reptile' after the bony plates along its back. Scientists think these probably helped to keep the dinosaur the right temperature. The spikes on the end of its tail would have been good for bashing unfriendly predators.

IGUANODON

Iguanodon could probably walk on either four legs or two. It had hands with five fingers, including a spiked thumb. This would have been very useful to fend off predators.

ANKYLOSAURUS

Herbivorous dinosaurs needed protection from the meat-eaters and this one was a bit like an armoured tank. It was covered in bony plates and had spines down its sides. It also had a heavy, club-like tail.

GENTLE GIANTS UNDER THE SEA

WHALE SHARK

Luckily for divers this biggest fish in the world only eats plankton and small fish. The largest one found was 13.5 metres (44 feet) long. Each one has a different pattern of yellow spots that helps researchers keep track of them.

BLUE WHALE

The blue whale can grow as long as a basketball court and is the largest animal ever to have lived on Earth. It weighs as much as 33 elephants and its blood vessels are so wide that a human could swim through them.

Manatee

Dugong

DUGONGS AND MANATEES

Long-ago stories about mermaids may be based on sailors seeing these shy and gentle creatures. They are also sometimes called 'sea-cows' because they graze on underwater grasses.

CETACEAN

is the word for a sea mammal that has to come up to the surface to breathe. Cetology is the study of whales, dolphins and porpoises.

NARWHAL

This amazing creature looks like a cross between a unicorn and a whale. The males have a huge tusk that is actually a very overgrown tooth. Some narwhals even have two of them.

BASKING SHARK

This mysterious but gentle creature feeds on plankton with its huge mouth. It can filter an Olympic swimming-pool's worth of water in two hours and can grow as long as a double-decker bus.

GIANT CLAM

These multi-coloured clams are the largest molluscs on Earth and can grow up to 1.2 metres (4 feet) across. No two clams are the same colour and they can live for up to 100 years. They open and close far too slowly to trap any divers!

HUMPHEAD WRASSE

An enormous coral reef fish that has a weird bump on its forehead. It can live for up to 30 years and change from being female to male and back again. It is really friendly to divers and will come up to be patted just like a dog.

LEATHERBACK TURTLE

This is the largest of the sea turtles and it has a leathery, rather than hard, shell. It eats a huge amount of jellyfish and sometimes mistakes discarded plastic bags for a tasty meal. This can be deadly for these endangered giants of the sea.

GLOW-IN-THE-DARK CREATURES

HEADLAMP BEETLE

A fantastic beetle with two glowing green lights on its back and an orange one that 'switches' on underneath the creature when it is about to take off.

FIREFLIES

These are not flies but beetles from the same family as glow-worms. They can fly and look like lots of fairy lights twinkling in the trees. Males flash at night and, if a female is impressed, she will flash back.

GLOW-WORMS

These are not really worms at all, but bioluminescent beetles with glowing tummies. The females glow to attract a mate and also to tell predators that glow-worms taste revolting.

CHIMPANZEE FIRE

Many kinds of fungi or mushrooms glow in the dark and this one is found in the forests of West and Central Africa. The fungi glow as they clean up the forest floor by eating dead leaves and vegetation.

TOXIC MILLIPEDES

In the mountains of California you can see greenish-blue millipedes glowing at night. Scientists think they do this as a warning to predators that they are not good to eat. They are very poisonous.

BIOLUMINESCENCE

is light made by living organisms to attract attention, frighten enemies, use as a disguise, or to find prey in the dark.

VAMPIRE SQUID

This scary-sounding creature can make a light show of flashing lights to scare off predators or attract prey. It lives really deep down in the ocean and has big, bright eyes too.

DEEP-SEA SHARKS

These sharks not only glow in the dark, but also have eyes that are adapted to take in as much light as possible down in the depths of the ocean. It means being able to spot each other, catch food and avoid predators.

WAVES OF LIGHT

Tiny, microscopic plants and animals in the sea, called plankton, can make the surface of the ocean glow and glint like a magical sea of light.

CRYSTAL JELLYFISH

Many jellyfish glow in the dark. When crystal jellyfish are disturbed they light up with a green glow around the rim of their bell shapes.

ANGLERFISH

A deep-sea fish that goes fishing with a glowing 'fishing rod'! It has a spine sticking up from the middle of its head that it can wriggle to look like bait. Then it grabs its prey with its huge mouth and long, pointed teeth.

HIGH-SPEED ANIMALS

RACEHORSE OF THE BUG WORLD

The ladybird is a very speedy bug. Scientists have found that ladybirds can travel at 60 kph (37 mph). That is as fast as a racehorse.

SUPER SWIFTS

Swifts are very well named, as they are superfast insect-eaters. Their wings are long and curved and the birds spend most of their time in the air. In fact they can even sleep on the wing.

CHARGING RHINO!

Black rhinos are huge creatures, but they are surprisingly fast on their feet. They can turn really quickly and reach speeds of 55 kph (34 mph).

SPEED ON SIX LEGS

Tiger beetles are really fierce hunters with long legs. Compared to their body size, it is like a human running at 770 kph (480 mph).

KILLER KICKERS

Ostriches are the world's largest bird. They cannot fly but can sprint at 70 kph (45 mph) and keep going at this speed for 30 minutes. Their legs are so strong that one kick can kill a human.

SPEEDY SWIMMER

The gentoo penguin cannot fly but it is probably the fastest swimming bird in the world. It can reach speeds of up to 36 kph (22 mph) and is better than other penguins at diving too.

KANGAROO STAMINA

Kangaroos are the only large animals that get about by hopping, but it does not stop them covering a lot of ground. Red kangaroos can keep going at 40 kph (25 mph) for about 2 kilometres (1.2 miles).

CURIOUS WORD

VELOCITY

means the speed and direction of an object or living creature.

HIGH-SPEED HUNTER

The peregrine falcon can dive at lightning speed to pounce on prey. When it dives or 'stoops' like this it can reach the incredible speed of 320 kph (200 mph).

LARGE BUT FAST

Wildebeests are part of the antelope family. They need to be able to move fast to escape from predators like lions and wild dogs. Calves can walk within minutes of birth and adults can reach speeds of 80 kph (50 mph) in an emergency.

TOP SPRINTER

The cheetah is the fastest animal on land. In 2012 a cheetah called Sarah was timed at Cincinnati Zoo running 100 metres in 5.95 seconds. Usain Bolt's record for the same distance is 9.58 seconds!

FAST FISH

It is hard to measure the speed of fish, but the sailfish has been estimated to jet through the water at nearly the same speed as a cheetah on land. It can flatten the huge fin on its back to be as streamlined as possible.

INGENIOUS HOMES FOR HUMANS

PALACE IN THE SKY

The stunning Summer Palace at Wadi Dhahr in Yemen was built on top of a huge rock in the 1920s. The owner could look down on everyone else!

TREEHOUSE PEOPLE

The Koroway tribe in Papua, Indonesia build treehouses up to 30 metres (98 feet) up in the jungle. Climbing the stairs means using a notched tree-trunk.

HOUSES ON A LAKE

Houses on Lake Inle in Burma (or Myanmar) are made of bamboo and stand like islands on wooden stilts in the water. They have floating gardens and fields. Children here learn to swim before they can walk.

PORTABLE HOUSES

The nomads of Mongolia have lived in yurts for thousands of years. These are made from a lattice made of willow or birch wood covered with thick felt. They can be taken down and put up really quickly.

LIVING ON THE SEABED

Deep-sea homes for humans are still really a dream of the future. Most of the people who have spent any time living deep down on the seabed are scientists in special units for research and exploration.

TROGLODYTE

means someone who
lives in a cave.

THE HANGING MONASTERY

This is a temple in China that
has been built high into a cliff.
It looks as if it will fall down at
any moment but it has been
there for at least 1,500 years.

CAVE HOMES

In the Loire Valley in France there are lots of
troglodyte houses carved straight into the rock.
Some of them have even been made into hotels,
wine cellars and restaurants.

BURROW TOWN

In the south of Australia
there is an opal-mining
town called Coober
Pedy where it is so hot in
summer that the miners
who live there have dug out
comfortable houses under
the ground. They call them
dugouts.

DESERT DWELLINGS

In a place called Matmata in Tunisia, North Africa, the
people have dug amazing homes under the desert.
They are cool in the day and keep them warm in the
chilly desert nights.

OFF-GRID LIVING

Some people try to live in houses that are not
connected to any electricity, gas or water supplies.
They use solar panels, wind turbines and rainwater
instead. To be truly off-grid you would have to give
up your mobile phone and the internet too!

POWERING THE PLANET

ENERGY FROM THE SUN

Heat and light from the Sun take just over 8 minutes to reach the Earth. Plants and trees use the energy in sunlight to make their own food.

GREENHOUSE GAS

Oil, coal and gas will not last for ever. Burning them makes a gas called carbon dioxide that traps the Sun's heat near Earth, creating what is called the Greenhouse Effect. Our climate seems to be changing because of this and we must find ways of slowing it down.

TIDAL ENERGY

The tide changes twice a day and the movement of the water can be used to turn generators that create electricity without producing harmful gases.

WATER POWER

Hydro-electricity is made by building a dam across a river or lake and then forcing the water down tunnels to turn turbines to make electricity. No harmful gases are created, but building a dam totally changes the environment nearby.

FOSSIL FUELS

Fossil fuels like oil, coal and gas were formed millions of years ago from the remains of dead plants and animals. Using them to make electricity and as fuel for cars causes pollution and the Greenhouse Effect.

WIND POWER

A wind turbine has propellers that turn in the wind to drive a machine called a generator that can make electricity. They do not make greenhouse gases, but need lots of wind and some people really do not like the look of them near their houses.

CURIOUS WORDS ↷

RENEWABLE

energy comes from things that do not run out, like the Sun or the sea.

NON-RENEWABLE

energy comes from sources that will run out. We cannot make any more of them.

NUCLEAR POWER

Uranium ore is made into a metal that can make a huge amount of electricity. The disadvantage is that it produces very dangerous radioactive waste that has to be stored very carefully.

FRACKING

Water, sand and chemicals are injected into shale rock to 'fracture' it and release the gas and oil inside it. There is a worry that the chemicals may be harmful, the process uses loads of water and it may cause small earthquakes.

SOLAR POWER

Solar panels, or photovoltaic cells, make electricity from the power of the Sun. The Sun will not run out soon, but it is expensive to build solar power stations and the panels cannot work if it is cloudy.

BIOMASS ENERGY

Electricity can be made from burning wood, plants and our old rubbish. It is a good way of using up waste, but burning it creates greenhouse gases. Growing trees to burn also takes up room where crops might be planted to feed people.

SPECIAL EFFECTS IN THE SKY

SOLAR ECLIPSE

Sometimes the Moon blocks out the light from the Sun. A total eclipse means that all of the light is blocked and the sky goes dark. All you can see of the Sun is glowing white gases like a halo around the black circle of the Moon. (You must never look at the Sun without eye protection.)

SPIDER LIGHTNING

This kind of lightning appears to crawl out of a cloud during a thunderstorm. It spreads across the sky like the branches of a tree. It is also called an 'anvil crawler'. Anvil clouds are thunderclouds.

FOG BOWS

These look like the ghosts of rainbows. They are almost white and not coloured like rainbows because the water droplets in the mist and fog are too small to turn the light into separate colours.

CONTRAILS

These are man-made clouds of ice crystals that form when water droplets in the air condense and freeze on particles in plane exhaust. Some of them last longer than others.

CURIOUS WORD ⇀

CREPUSCULE

means the time of day just after sunset. Other words for it are dusk or twilight.

THE MILKY WAY

The Milky Way is our home galaxy. There are billions of galaxies in the Universe with gigantic numbers of stars in each one. On dark, clear nights it is possible to see the Milky Way looking like a wide band of white dust stretching across the sky.

AURORA BOREALIS

This is a wonderful show of coloured lights in the night sky also known as the Northern Lights as they are most common in Arctic regions. They are caused by tiny pieces from the Sun crashing into the Earth's atmosphere high above the North Pole.

MOON HALO

Ice crystals in clouds high up above the Earth can make the Moon look as if it has a halo around it. A Moon halo can often be a sign of stormy weather to come.

LUNAR ECLIPSE

This is when the Earth comes between the Sun and the Moon. The Earth's shadow can be seen crossing the Moon. The Moon looks a lot darker and reddish but it does not disappear completely.

LIGHT PILLARS

These columns of light stretch up or down from sources of light including the Sun, Moon or even streetlamps. They are caused by the light bouncing off ice crystals in the air.

RARE CLOUDS

Noctilucent, or night-shining, clouds are Earth's highest clouds. They form on ice crystals and dust near the edge of space. They appear after sunset and look very alien with their ripples of bright blue across the sky.

UNEXPECTED INGREDIENTS

TREES → PAPER

Most of the paper we use is made from trees. The wood is chopped up and then soaked and ground into a pulp. This is treated with chemicals and dyes before being pressed and dried into sheets of paper. The sheets are rolled up and cut to size.

SAND → GLASS

Sand is mixed with other ingredients, such as soda and lime, and then heated to a very high temperature. This makes a liquid that can be moulded or blown into anything from windowpanes to beautiful glass ornaments.

OIL → MAKE-UP

Crude oil is a fossil fuel that has many uses. It is made into petrol, diesel and fuel for aeroplanes. Chemicals from processing the oil are also used in the making of many beauty products such as skin creams and make-up.

SEAWEED → TOOTHPASTE

You need to be able to squeeze your toothpaste out of its tube. Seaweed contains something called carrageenan that is added to the paste to make it the right thickness. Seaweed extracts can also be added to ice-cream to make it smooth and stop ice crystals from forming.

TREE LIQUID → TYRES

The liquid from rubber trees is called latex. The trees are cut and the milky-white latex flows into small buckets. It can be made into all kinds of useful things like tyres, hoses, rubber bands, gloves and ducks for bath time!

MANUFACTURE

comes from two Latin words: manus = hand, facere = to make. Most manufacturing is done in factories these days!

DIAMONDS → DRILLS

Diamonds are extremely hard and do not melt easily. This means they can be used as drill-heads for powering through rocks, bricks and concrete, for example on oil rigs.

CATERPILLAR COCOONS → SILK

Silk is a beautiful fabric woven from an unusual thread that comes from the cocoons of silkworms. These are not worms at all but the caterpillars of the silk moth. They munch away on mulberry leaves before spinning their cocoons of fine thread.

BUGS → RED SWEETS

SILVER → BANDAGES

Silver is very good at fighting off bacteria that cause infection. Many medical instruments are made using silver. Bandages with just a small amount of silver in them can help wounds to heal more quickly.

Next time you pop a red sweet into your mouth think about how it got its red colour. Red food dyes, called cochineal and carmine, are made out of ground-up insects. They are added to many pink or red-coloured foods and cosmetics.

WHIZZY STUFF IN THE GALAXIES

SPACE TELESCOPES

These satellites are used to look at the planets and stars. The Hubble Space Telescope can see further into space than telescopes on the ground, but it is difficult and expensive to launch and, if anything goes wrong, only astronauts can fix it.

SPACE PROBES

Space probes do not have humans on board. They can travel for years to other planets or moons to collect and send back scientific information. Some space probes go into orbit around other planets, some land on them and others leave our Solar System to explore far into space.

METEORS

There are little chunks of rock in space called meteoroids. When they reach the Earth's atmosphere they get really hot and burn up, looking like amazing fireworks streaking across the sky. These are called meteors or, sometimes, shooting stars.

ARTIFICIAL SATELLITES

These are launched into space by rockets. They go round (orbit) the Earth and are used for communications, sending television and phone signals, for watching the weather, for helping us navigate the planet and for spying!

METEORITE

When a meteor hits the Earth it is called a meteorite. Some of them have made huge holes, or craters, in the ground. In Arizona, USA there is a massive one over 1 kilometre wide.

CELESTIAL

is a word used to describe things in the sky or outer space. Planets and stars are celestial bodies.

BLACK HOLE

This may form after a star has exploded. It is a very tight ball of gas that has such a huge pull of gravity that it even sucks light into it.

NEBULAE

Nebulae are enormous gas clouds in space where stars are born. Stars are huge balls of burning gas. As the stars get bigger, the nebulae begin to glow. The nearest star to Earth is the Sun.

RED GIANT

Stars burn for billions of years, but then they begin to run out of gas. They then change from white to red, grow bigger and become red giants.

SUPERNOVA

Other red giants get bigger and bigger until there is gigantic explosion called a supernova.

WHITE DWARF

Some red giants slowly shrink and become stars that are called white dwarfs.

COMETS

These are great big dirty ice balls that can be several kilometres across. If they come close to the Sun the ice in them melts and creates a tail of dust and gas. Halley's Comet can be seen from Earth every 75-76 years. Its next visit will be 2061.

TECHNOLOGY IN THE CITY

LIFTS

The first powered lifts for people were invented in the 19th century, as buildings grew taller. The Taipei 101 building in Taiwan has a very fast lift that can go from the 5th to 89th floor in 37 seconds.

Burj Khalifa

FIRST RECORD-BREAKER

The Empire State Building in New York was the world's tallest building when it was first built in 1931. The lightning rod that protects the building is struck by lightning about 23 times every year.

MONORAIL TRAINS

These are trains that run on just one rail or concrete track. They usually travel high above the street level and this means they avoid traffic jams in busy cities. They are also easier to build than new underground lines.

SKYSCRAPERS

Skyscrapers are built using a very strong steel framework to carry the massive weight of the building. This 'skeleton' is anchored deep into the ground. Steel girders form the floors between the steel columns.

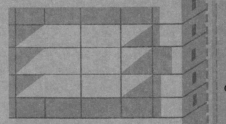

COMPUTER DESIGN

Like many recent and unusual buildings, the Gherkin in London was built using computer-aided design, or CAD. CAD helps the people who plan buildings, the architects, to check that their ideas will actually work.

STANDING UP TO THE WIND

More than 40 wind tunnel tests had to be carried out to make sure the Burj Khalifa in Dubai would stand up to the wind. The tower stands 828 metres (2,717 feet) high and even has a swimming-pool on its 76th floor.

INFRASTRUCTURE

is the word used to describe the system of roads, buildings, power and communications that make a city work.

SELF-CLEANING GLASS

Many modern skyscrapers are built with windows made from self-cleaning glass. The glass has a special coating on it to prevent dirt from sticking to it

ESCALATORS

These moving staircases transport people up and down in shopping malls, stations and other large buildings. In the Moscow Metro there is one escalator that is so long you cannot see the top when you are at the bottom. It takes three minutes, or long enough to boil an egg, to ride it.

CLEVER LIGHTS

Many cities now use a kind of light bulb called an LED in streetlights. They do not use much energy and last for a long time. Modern lights can also be set up so that they get brighter when people and traffic are there, and dimmer if the street is empty.

SMART CITIES

Streetlamps can also have other gadgets called sensors attached to them. These can take in information about all sorts of things like the weather, pollution and noise.

UNDERGROUND TRAINS

The first underground train system opened in London in 1863 with steam trains. Technology has, of course, improved since then and some metro systems in the world now even use trains without drivers.

HOW AIRPORTS WORK

FIREFIGHTERS

Airports have their own special firefighters on hand. Some fire engines have hoses with nozzles that can break through the side of an aircraft. They are called 'snozzles'!

CHECKING-IN AND BOARDING

The people we show our tickets to are called passenger handling agents or passenger service agents. They weigh and label our luggage and also check our boarding passes just before we get on the plane.

AIRPORT VETS

Animals have to travel in special crates and are usually put in the cargo hold. Airports have trained animal handlers and vets to look after them.

CURIOUS WORD

AERODROME

is a landing area for planes that is not as large as an airport. An aerodrome is mainly used by smaller aircraft.

CUSTOMS OFFICERS

These officers check that passengers are not bringing anything forbidden, or illegal, into a country. They search luggage and use sniffer dogs to help them.

AIRFIELD OPERATIONS

The people working on the airfield make sure that the runways are safe. They check for holes, clear ice and snow and scare birds away with loud noises.

AIR TRAFFIC CONTROL

Air traffic controllers sit in a control tower and instruct pilots on their speed, height and route. They work 24 hours a day and must not make a mistake.

GROUND SERVICES

The ground crew handles mountains of suitcases every day, getting them transported on to and off planes. They also direct, or marshal, the planes on and off the stands where they are parked.

IMMIGRATION OFFICERS

Every international airport has immigration officers to check passengers' passports. They can ask why they are travelling to a country and must look out for any suspicious behaviour.

SECURITY

Airport security officers x-ray baggage to make sure it does not contain anything dangerous like knives, guns or bombs. They also ask people to go through special metal-detecting gates.

PILOTS AND CABIN CREW

There are usually two pilots on a plane, a captain and a first officer. The flight attendants, or cabin crew, look after the passengers.

THE PAINTER'S TOOLKIT

CAVE PAINTERS

No one really knows why prehistoric humans made cave paintings. They made paints out of red, yellow, black and brown rocks and earth. They probably used hollowed-out bones to blow the paint on the walls, sometimes using their own hands as a kind of stencil.

WATERCOLOURS AND GOUACHE

Watercolours are transparent, water-based paints in tubes or solid blocks called 'pans'. They are ideal for painting using layers of colour. Gouache is similar, but chalk is added to the pigments to make it opaque rather than transparent.

PAINTING WITH EGGS

Before oil paints, artists used a kind of fast-drying paint called egg tempera. It was made from mixing ground-up colours, or pigments, with egg yolk. It had to be made freshly each time it was needed.

PORTABLE KIT

The first oil paints had to be mixed each time you needed them. In the 1840s, oils in metal tubes were invented. With folding easels and small canvases this meant that painters could paint wherever they liked, and especially outside in the countryside.

CANVAS AND OTHER SURFACES

A canvas is made from a rough cotton or linen cloth, usually stretched across a wooden frame. Painters also paint on walls, wood, paper and sometimes metal, glass, slate or even themselves!

CURIOUS WORD →

CHIAROSCURO

is an Italian word used to describe the contrasting effects of light and shade in a painting.

OIL PAINTS

By the 1500s artists were using paints made by mixing colours with linseed or walnut oil. Oil paint dries slowly and is ideal for painting on canvas. It can be used for delicate shading or wonderful gloopy, thick effects.

ART ON A SCREEN

Modern technology means that some artists use a tablet computer to create a painting. It is easy to make changes and alter the colours as they go along.

BRUSHES AND PALETTE KNIVES

Brushes are made from all kinds of natural animal or man-made hair. Bristly brushes are best for oil paints, but fine, soft brushes are needed for watercolours. A palette knife is used for mixing paint but it can also be good for putting oil paints on to a canvas.

NOT PAINT!

Some modern artists, like Picasso, make paintings using all kinds of other materials like bits of newspaper, catalogues, old string and rope. An artist called Anselm Kiefer uses straw, mud and even diamonds with paint to create an artwork.

MEGA MACHINES

SUPERTANKERS

These are the largest ships in the world. They carry liquid cargo like oil across the oceans. They are so huge that it can take them up to 10 kilometres (6 miles) to stop!

CRUISE LINERS

The largest cruise liners are like small floating towns for several thousand holidaymakers. They have restaurants, shops, cinemas, theatres, tennis courts, spas and swimming-pools.

BENDY BUSES

These are like two buses stuck together. Only one driver is needed and they can carry more people around crowded cities and towns. Some even longer buses are being invented!

ARTICULATED LORRIES

The biggest lorries have a separate engine and cab for the driver. This is called a tractor. All kinds of trailers for carrying loads can be attached at the back. Some of them are enormous.

CARGO CRANES

Huge metal boxes, or containers, are used to transport all sorts of goods all over the world. Massive cranes lift them on and off gigantic container ships.

TOWER CRANES

These giants are essential for lifting the heavy materials used to build skyscrapers. The crane operator sits in a little cabin high up above the ground.

GIANT BORING MACHINES

These are used to make tunnels for new train lines or routes under rivers or through mountains. Some of these mighty machines even have their own toilet and kitchen for the crew.

GIANT MIXERS

Loads of concrete is needed on building sites. The mixers fetch sand, cement and gravel from a factory. The drum keeps turning as they drive along to mix the concrete and stop it from going hard.

EXCAVATORS

These powerful mega-diggers are used to excavate trenches and holes, and to clear rubble and earth. The driver sits in a cab that can turn a complete circle.

CURIOUS WORD

MECHANICAL

is the word used to describe the way that engines and machines work.

WRITING AROUND THE WORLD

ALPHABETS

An alphabet is a way of writing down what we say (our language), using letters for each sound. The word 'alphabet' comes from the first two letters of the ancient Greek alphabet 'alpha' (=a) and 'beta' (=b).

PHOENICIAN ALPHABET

About 3,000 years ago, the Phoenicians who lived around the Mediterranean Sea created an alphabet with 22 letters. It was much easier to use than some other early forms of writing. The Greek, Roman, Arabic and Hebrew alphabets all developed from this.

ROMAN WRITING

The Romans used an alphabet similar to the ancient Greek one. As they marched across Europe they brought it with them. In Britain, France, Italy, Spain, Portugal and many other countries it is still used today.

ANCIENT GREEK

The ancient Greeks improved the Phoenician alphabet by adding letters for vowel sounds (a, e, i, o, u). It made everything much easier to understand. However, they still did not have any commas or full stops and there were no gaps between any of the words!

```
A B C D E F
G H I K L M
N O P Q R S
T V X Y Z
```

English	Hello
French	Bonjour
Spanish	¡Hola!
Italian	Ciao
Portuguese	Olá

Hello
marhaba
مرحبا

ARABIC

Arabic is written and read from right to left across the page. It is used all over the Arab world in countries such as Algeria, Egypt, Saudi Arabia and Iraq.

CURIOUS WORD ⤵

MANUSCRIPT

comes from the Latin 'manus' (hand) and 'scriptum' (writing). A manuscript was a book written by hand before the invention of printing.

Hello
zdravstvuj
здравствуй

CYRILLIC ALPHABET

This alphabet grew out of the Greek alphabet. It is used by people in countries like Russia, Bulgaria and Serbia to write down their languages.

Hello
shalom
שלום

HEBREW

Like Arabic, Hebrew is written and read from right to left. It is the language used in Israel and by Jewish people all over the world.

Hello
namastē
नमस्ते

DEVANAGARI ALPHABET

This is the main alphabet of northern India and is used to write down Hindi and other Indian languages. It is also sometimes called the Nagari alphabet.

Hello
ni hao
你好

Hello
annyeonghaseyo
안녕하세요

KOREAN WRITING

Korean is written down using characters for each syllable in a word. It is said that King Sejong of Korea invented this writing system in the fifteenth century. It is called Hangul, a word with two syllables written like this:

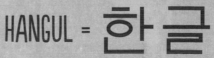

HANGUL = 한글

CHINESE CHARACTERS

Chinese is one of the oldest kinds of writing that is still used by people today. It uses characters rather than letters of an alphabet. These characters stand for things or ideas. Chinese children have to learn thousands of these characters at school.

TOYS IN TIME

JIGSAW MAPS

Early jigsaws were maps stuck on to wood and cut into simple pieces. In 1870 a type of saw called a jig saw was invented. This could cut puzzle pieces into the more complicated curved shapes that we have today.

DINKY HOUSES

The first dolls' houses in the 1550s were called 'baby houses'. Rich grown-ups used them to show off their beautiful miniature treasures. Luckily, during the next century, toymakers began to build dolls' houses for children.

CUDDLY TEDDIES

Teddy bears were named after the American President Theodore (or Teddy) Roosevelt. He refused to shoot a bear when he was on a hunting trip in 1902. Toymakers started making 'Teddy' bears and everyone wanted one!

MARBLE MANIA

Roman children had marbles made of glass, pottery or polished nuts. More recently, when 'glass scissors' were invented in 1846, marbles were made by cutting pieces off long glass rods.

CURIOUS WORD ⤍

ARCTOPHILE

is someone who loves teddy bears and likes to collect them.

ANCIENT YO-YOS

Yo-yos have been around for a very long time. Even the Ancient Greeks had them. In about 1789 there was a yo-yo craze in Europe when the yo-yo was called a 'quiz' or 'bandalore'.